ISBN 978-1-397-33021-5
PIBN 11374327

1 MONTH OF
FREE
READING

at

www.ForgottenBooks.com

By purchasing this book you are eligible for one month membership to ForgottenBooks.com, giving you unlimited access to our entire collection of over 1,000,000 titles via our web site and mobile apps.

To claim your free month visit: www.forgottenbooks.com/free1374327

English
Français
Deutsche
Italiano
Español
Português

www.forgottenbooks.com

Mythology Photography **Fiction**
Fishing Christianity **Art** Cooking
Essays Buddhism Freemasonry
Medicine **Biology** Music **Ancient**
Egypt Evolution Carpentry Physics
Dance Geology **Mathematics** Fitness
Shakespeare **Folklore** Yoga Marketing
Confidence Immortality Biographies
Poetry **Psychology** Witchcraft
Electronics Chemistry History **Law**
Accounting **Philosophy** Anthropology
Alchemy Drama Quantum Mechanics
Atheism Sexual Health **Ancient History**
Entrepreneurship Languages Sport
Paleontology Needlework Islam
Metaphysics Investment Archaeology
Parenting Statistics Criminology
Motivational

PHYSICAL TRAINING IN NEW ENGLAND SCHOOLS,

BY

W. SCOTT, A. M., Secretary of New England Education League,

WITH LETTERS FROM

New England State Secretaries of Education, City Superintendents, Principals of High and Endowed Schools, College Gymnasium Directors, New York City and Philadelphia City Superintendents, and Gymnastic Teacher at West Point.

THE APOLLO BELVEDERE.

THE PEOPLE PUBLISHING COMPANY,
10 HOLLIS STREET,
CAMBRIDGE, MASS.
1899.

This address and inquiry were prepared under the auspices of the New England Education League. They were given before the Boston Physical Education Society at Rogers Building, Boston, Mass., at the February meeting, 1899, and before the High School Teachers' Institute in Hall of Representatives, Concord, N. H., April 28, 1899.

The following photographs and other material were used at the institute: English school views, Phillips-Exeter gymnasium, athletic field and athletics, Boston Normal School of Gymnastics, Harvard fields and athletic groups, Boston public gymnasia, swimming places, baths, classes, etc., New York City public school gymnasia, Cambridge and Rindge fields, Cambridge New Latin School with plans, Massachusetts State Normal School gymnasia, Gymnasia of Hartford High School, Wilbraham Academy, etc., Yale gymnasium and prescription of exercises, Manual of New Haven public schools, Connecticut manual of hygiene, etc., Greek statuary.

PHYSICAL TRAINING IN NEW ENGLAND SCHOOLS.

Man made the school, God made the playground. Before letters were invented or books, or governesses discovered, the neighbors' children, the outdoor life, the fists and the wrestling sinews, the old games (the oldest things in the world), the bare hill and the clear river,—these were education; and now, though Xenophon and sums be come, these are and remain. Horses and marbles, the knot of boys beside the schoolboy fire, the hard blows given and the harder ones received,—these educate mankind.

WALTER BAGEHOT.

Home training needs a reinforcement in the form of supervision on the streets and playgrounds. Public playgrounds, well conducted by skilled and experienced teachers, should be authorized and maintained by the city authorities, and patronized and attended as regularly as the schools.

FRANZ SCHOEBERLE.

I have come to the conclusion that more than half the disease which embitters the middle and latter part of life is due to avoidable errors in diet.

SIR HENRY THOMPSON.

Or know ye not that your body is a temple of the Holy Ghost?

PAUL (1 Cor. 6:19).

One of the first things to be regarded in the pupil as school work begins is physical health and condition. No right system of education will ignore this important matter at any stage of the pupil's progress. Public education too often has neglected this subject or failed to give to it the attention it requires. In some private schools and colleges it has been lifted to a proper place on an equality with other departments of training. The tendency of school life and public opinion are setting in the right direction, but more emphasis needs to be put on proper care of the pupil's health and physical state. It is not sufficient to keep pupils from breaking down under the pressure of school life. Many who do not go to that extreme come from the schools as weaklings for the work of life. A still larger number fail to receive that bodily development which is one of the best equipments for after life.

Nor are teachers and parents wholly responsible for such results. In some cases they are doubtless remiss, but the chief difficulty lies in the inadequate recognition of physical training in public education and the lack or weakness of public opinion on the subject. The supervision of trained instructors is essential to physical culture. They should have special knowledge, experience and intelligent sympathy with the work. A physical director should understand not merely the physical side of youth but the complex relations of mind and body. Thus he may be in accord with the best ideals of the school and may contribute to laying such a sound physical basis as will sustain the mental and moral structure to be reared thereon.

Searching physical examinations to show the condition of the pupil and his ability to do the school work are necessary at proper times. The eye which is not unfrequently impaired in school life, the ear upon which so many calls are daily made, especially need occasional examinations.* Ques-

* The writer finds, in frequent visits to city and country schools, light entering schoolrooms in a way to impair sight of teachers and pupils.

tions of food, exercise, care of body, the bath, habit, dress, rest, which have much to do with health and vigor and successful study, require appropriate treatment. Objections to certain kinds of sport and excess in them will be modified or removed under proper supervison.

The occupations of the school should be so conducted as to promote good bodily development. School life should not merely prevent the impairment of health, it should improve health. To impart knowledge or to develop the mind at the expense of the bodily health is a perversion of effort to be carefully avoided. School life is made too sedentary in many cases, its drain on nerve and brain too excessive. Johann Peter Frank, the father of school hygiene, raised a warning a century ago against a premature strain on the youthful powers of body and mind: "Yet spare their fibres—spare their mind's strength; waste not upon the child the vigor of the man that is to be."

An interesting paper by Mr. Curtis of Clark University in the *Seminary* of October, 1898, treats this subject at much length. He asserts that the general average of school time is in excess of double the child's capacity on an average for lessons requiring mental effort. He cites cases to show that pupils on half school time with the rest given to work in garden or shop show equal or better results than full time pupils.

Physical training is advocated also as preventive of many physical evils in schools. As an example a portion of a report from *New York* city schools is quoted. Medical supervision by a corps of one hundred and fifty physicians began in 1897. The first day, March 29, 1897, gave the following results:

140 children excluded.
14 cases diphtheria.
3 cases measles.
1 scarlet fever.
35 contagious eye diseases.
3 mumps.

1 croup.
8 chicken pox.
8 skin diseases.
67 parasitic diseases.

Cases of neglect of cleanliness were numerous.

"We consider," say the members of the Brooklyn, N. Y., Homœopathic Medical Society, "the curriculum of the Girls' High School and the upper grammar grades too severe and exacting. The individual members of the committee have recently had under treatment many cases of nervous prostration among the attendants of the high school, which have been the direct result of faithful application to the required course of study, and the oculists have had their attention particularly directed to many cases from this school where the pupils are compelled to wear glasses, perhaps for life, because of the strain put upon the eyes and nervous system by the pressure."

The first fundamental research into the physical and mental health of school children was instituted by Dr. Hertel in Copenhagen in 1881, and it led to a special hygienic commission to examine the condition of health in all the schools of the kingdom of Denmark. At the same time a grand school commission was named in Sweden to inquire into the organization of school life. About 15,000 boys and 3,000 girls were examined in reference to health, measurement and weight. Professor Axel Key, a member of the Swedish commission, in an address before the Berlin International Congress speaks as follows:*

"According to my examinations of 15,000 boys in the middle schools more than one-third are ill or are afflicted with chronic maladies. Shortsightedness, which is demonstrably for the most part induced by the overtaxing of the eyes is school work, and well merits the name of school sickness, rises rapidly in height of preva-

* "School Life in Relation to Growth and Health," by Prof. Axel Key. *Popular Science Monthly*, Vol. XXXVIII, pp. 107-112. Year 1890-91.

lence from class to class. Thirteen and a half per cent of the boys suffer from habitual headache, and nearly thirteen per cent are pallid; and other diseases arise in the lower classes to decline and rise again in the upper classes. Diseases of the lungs are most frequent among organic disorders. Diseases of the heart and intestinal disorders show a considerable tendency to increase in the higher classes. As to the average of illness in the different classes, it appears that in Stockholm seventeen per cent of the children in the first class were ill at the end of the first year. In the second school year the illness curve rose to thirty-seven per cent and in the fourth class to forty per cent. This remarkable increase of illness during the first school year is not casual, but it is exhibited in all the schools; and corresponding conditions were brought to light in the examinations of Danish pupils. A sickness ratio of 34.4 per cent was found as early as in the lowest classes of the middle schools."

"The most healthy of all the years of youth is with boys the seventeenth, which is also one of the two years of most active growth. The eighteenth, on the contrary, which follows immediately on the attainment of puberty, appears to be a very unhealthy period."

"Among the schoolgirls, the future mothers of generations to come, investigation instituted in thirty-five schools with 3,072 pupils brought out a fearful amount of illness. Sixty-one per cent of the whole, all belonging to the well-to-do classes, were ill or afflicted with serious chronic disorders; thirty-six per cent were suffering from chlorosis, and as many from habitual headache; at least ten per cent had spinal disorder, etc. . . . The explanation of it is easily found in the method of instruction for girls as a whole, and in the organization of girls' schools after the pattern of boys' schools. The amount of work, sitting still, etc., exacted of the girl is not consistent with her health during her growing time. Without going into particulars as to the influences injurious to the health of growing children which proceed ·from their homes or may be brought out in connection with the school and school work, it is still manifest that the burden of work which children have to bear under recent school regulations far exceeds what is permissible, and is to a large extent responsible for the liability of school children to illness."

The same authority calls attention to the periods of growth in boys and girls, and to the differences in growth at various months of the year as having a bearing on arrangement of vacations and school management.

A few words as to the physical surroundings of the school to promote health and right bodily development must suffice here.

Every school or group of schools should have a playground and use it under proper supervision. In our variable climate indoor playrooms or gymnasiums are also essential. The best sanitary conditions, ventilation, dining or lunch room, baths, sanitaries found in the most carefully arranged schools should be universal.

Take the playground. Teachers interested in the sports of youth as sources of pleasure and educational opportunity often quote Wellington's saying as he looked on the playground of Eton College, "There Waterloo was won." But the backs of Eton are large enough for the evolutions of an army. The playground has relation to bodily development, to spontaneity of action, power of initiative physically and mentally and thus affects the spirit and vigor of the future society.

It is often said playgrounds, however desirable, are expensive especially in cities. But we reply, the difficulty does not rest at that point. Every city has open spaces, small and large parks and park systems, but by an ingenuity that will surprise the future student of our times these have been kept away from the schools of the people.

The parkman and the schoolman, going forth to teach and adorn the city, have started back to back and the farther they have gone the greater the distance between them. We have a park system and a school system but they are quite distinct. The failure of schoolmen to secure right relations between these systems, the lack of concert of action in departments of city government and unformed public opinion have deprived school children of playgrounds. It has not been a matter of cost. One of the best things in childhood and school life, the joy and discipline of innocent play, has thus been largely lost. These conditions should be quickly changed.

We might dwell on other physical features of the school which touch the subject in hand, but will venture simply to note one more, the bath.

The idea of ample bathing facilities in schoolhouses seems strange to many people, but the fact that it so appears illustrates the failure of the school property to stand in right relations to the physical side of education and the community. Dr. Rohe of Baltimore, in a recent address before the American Medical Association, gave statistics of eighteen American cities with no free public baths. Among these were Cambridge,* Mass., Portland, Me., Baltimore, Cincinnati, Milwaukee, Minneapolis, St. Louis. His conclusion was that "five-sixths of the inhabitants of these cities have no facilities for bathing, except such as are afforded by pail and sponge, or river, lake or other body of water which may be accessible, but in winter even such sources of cleanliness are cut off." Dr. T. M. Balliet, superintendent of schools of Springfield, Mass., advocating school baths in that city asserts that only one-half of the families have bath rooms in their homes. He also shows that lack of cleanliness in school children in clothing or person pollutes the air, offends the sense of smell, injures the nerve centres and diffuses infective germs.

* Cambridge new Latin School has ample bathing facilities, playroom, gymnasium, bicycle rooms, etc.

Mr. H. G. Wadlin, chief of the Bureau of Statistics for Labor in Massachusetts, in his report a few years ago, affirms in reference to Boston that in 1892 a little above one-fourth of the people, living in rented houses, had proper bathing facilities and nearly three-fourths had none. Dr. E. M. Hartwell in his addresses has stated that in many cities of Germany, Switzerland and Scandinavia the bath has become a most useful adjunct of schools.

Physical training involves better physical conditions in school properties, a wiser adjustment of school life and work to the health and development of pupils. The public is ready to coöperate with such a cause. A pure, sound body has a close connection with the mental and moral elevation and the future vigor of the race.

We pass now to an inquiry into the present state of physical training in the schools of New England.

The writer has collected brief statements from the following quarters:

I. State secretaries of education in New England.
II. City superintendents in representative cities.
III. Principals of prominent high schools.
IV. Principals of leading endowed secondary schools.
V. College gymnasium directors.
VI. City superintendents in New York and Philadelphia.
VII. West Point Military Academy.

The results of the inquiry are submitted with the wish that it might have been more exhaustive, but the writer has been unable to go into the investigation more fully at this time. For our present purpose it is perhaps sufficiently complete.

The questions sent out were, in general, as follows:

1. What is the attitude of your institution (city, state) to physical training?
2. What specific methods are taken in connection with the subject?

3. How, in your opinion, may good physical training be secured in all public schools of the state?

The replies are summarized.

STATE OF MAINE.

Hon. W. W. Stetson, State Secretary of Education:*

Attitude favorable, Ling system used somewhat, public opinion is an effective way to secure a state system. It is not a legal subject.

Miss Mary S. Snow, City Superintendent, Bangor, Me.:

Attitude very friendly, Swedish system, Maine is a big rural state and it is hard to say how the state may be covered.

Albro E. Chase, Principal High School, Portland:

Attitude favorable. Teacher of recitations devotes one period per week to such work as may aid her in her subject. Owing to conditions beyond control, physical training, in my judgment, cannot be secured in more than a few high schools in this state.

Professor W. B. Mitchell, Bowdoin College, Brunswick:

Believes such training should be in all public schools; thinks a system with music desirable for younger pupils. The Sargent system is used successfully at Bowdoin. End desired best attained, not by state laws, but by enthusiastic efforts of those interested. Teachers, superintendents and parents can have it, if desired; sends pamphlet of Dr. Whittier, the gymnasium director, advocating physical training.

STATE OF NEW HAMPSHIRE.

Hon. Channing Folsom, State Secretary of Education:

Physical training and method left to local authorities. I do not know

*A careful digest of letters is presented, but quotation marks are omitted, because nearly all letters are shortened.

how it may be secured in all public schools. It is not a legal subject.

F. H. Pease, Superintendent of Schools, Dover, N. H.:

Attitude favorable. Each teacher is required to give two periods of five minutes each daily to gymnastic exercises of some kind, the kind is left to teacher's choice. No regular voice training but many teachers use some form of training. Teachers should be trained in any one of the "best" systems which might extend throughout the city. Several systems might be used in the state. Correct standing, walking, etc., should be demanded. Athletics appeal to many boys, graceful carriage to many girls. The personality of the teacher counts for much.

T. W. Harris, Superintendent of Schools, Keene, N. H.:

City has no particular attitude to subject. Ling system was put into schools some years ago, five minutes or so of such exercise in middle of afternoon session. It is useful relaxation but has no special relation to physical development. Unless exercise is systematic with gymnasium and considerable attention given to it, it seems more a fad than anything else. Outdoor sports are many. No complaint of lack of physical exercise outside of school hours.

John F. Kent, Principal of High School, Concord, N. H.:

Attitude favorable, military drill for boys and girls.

Rev. J. H. Coit, St. Paul's School, Concord, N. H.:

Physical culture a special feature from beginning of school in 1856, promoted judiciously and carefully by all means in our power. Gymnastic classes in winter; ordinary games, athletic sports, rowing, boxing, fencing under guidance of experienced and competent masters.

Principal H. P. Amen, Phillips-Exeter Academy, Exeter, N. H.:

Our attitude thoroughly sympathetic, have a well trained director giving all his time to the work. Object is all around body building, required from middle of fall term to spring term. Each class has special exercises and in the four years receives systematic training. Four hours per week in physical work required from each student, half of each period given to class work and half to individual work, with careful physical examination. This subject counts as much as any other four-hour subject for graduation; no student admitted to the school who is unable to take regular gymnasium work. In no part of our work is there a stronger interest than in gymnasium work. It gives outlet for youthful spirits and ...., and contributes to moral character. Only men of a solid type and wide acquirements should be chosen to direct such work.

STATE OF VERMONT.

Hon. M. S. Stone, State Secretary of Education of Vermont:

Attitude favorable, mild gymnastic exercises used. May be extended over the state by stimulating teachers with a knowledge of the needs. It is not a legal subject.

Henry O. Wheeler, City Superintendent of Schools, Burlington, Vt.:

Physical culture does not hold the place it should occupy. Exercises have been used for years but irregularly. I believe in physical training in our schools, but have not seen my way to introduce it.

STATE OF MASSACHUSETTS.

Hon. F. A. Hill, State Secretary of Education:

The State Board believes schools should have good sanitary conditions and appropriate bodily exercises. In normal schools teachers are trained with these things in view. The school committees in progressive places are wide awake in these lines. Teachers generally have exercise of some sort, but probably many lack training for this work. Refers to cities, as Newton, Brookline, Boston. The normal graduate ought to carry into her work some good ideas on the subject. The normal schools one of the most effective ways of reaching the schools of the state. If hereafter every new teacher in Massachusetts should be required to have some minimum of professional training, including physical culture, that would be the most direct way of making physical culture general. Physical culture is a permissive subject by state law of 1897. Physiology, anatomy and hygiene are mandatory, and it would be a reasonable interpretation to include under a practical application of these subjects right bodily exercises. Attention has been specially called to the subject in my last annual report at some length and also in earlier reports.

C. F. Carroll, Superintendent of Schools, Worcester, Mass.:

Attitude favorable in and outside of public schools. A director instructs teachers and occasionally visits schools. Some division of the Board has existed in the past, but now there is no opposition. This plan is quite satisfactory. City or town teachers might be trained by a competent person. I favor physical culture for children of all ages, at least above the second and third grades. Even in primary and kindergarten grades there should be suitable physical training.

T. M. Balliet, Superintendent ? Schools, Springfield, Mass.:

Attitude friendly, each teacher ...s such physical training as she i. .....iar with. Physical training ..y be secured by getting a medic... .an who also understands physical training as a specialty to s..ervise it, and an assistant or c.... of assistants to train the teacher. We shall probably do this another year.

F. W. Atkinson, Principal of High School, Springfield, Mass.:

No provision unfortunately has been made even in our superb building for physical culture. It should be made compulsory, especially in the large cities. Our girls need physical training sadly.

D. W. Abercrombie, Principal of Worcester Academy, Worcester, Mass.:

"A sound mind in a sound body" is a working maxim of the school, and to secure it our best intelligence is directed. Encouragement is given to athletics, especially football and track athletics. Gymnasium work is required from Thanksgiving to May. Careful physical examinations are given to each boy and special work prescribed where needed. Classes meet three times per week and work is progressive. A class competition is held annually in March, not as an exhibition but as an exposition of the season's work.

Rev. Endicott Peabody, Head Master of Groton School, Groton, Mass.:

We have had much benefit from physical culture; pupils gain unusual development in measurement and strength. Our instructor has had special training for his work. It seems an excellent idea to secure physical training in all schools of the state. A state appropriation would bring it about, for there is no difficulty in discovering good teachers.

Dr. D. A. Sargent, Hemenway Gymnasium, Harvard University:

I regret that I have not the time to go into an extended discussion of the important question that you raise as to the "Correlation of Physical Culture to Public Education." My only answer to your questions is this: put physical culture on exactly the same footing in every respect and detail as you would mental culture in our public schools and colleges.

President C. W. Emerson, College of Oratory, Boston, Mass.:

Physical culture may be secured in the public schools of the state by having the right system selected, and by setting apart a portion of each day for its study and practice, the same as for other recitations.

STATE OF RHODE ISLAND.

Hon. T. B. Stockwell, State Commissioner of Public Schools:

The subject receives more attention from year to year; four of the five cities and at least five of the towns have special teachers. There are no uniform methods used; to secure good physical training in schools the regular teachers must be qualified to do the work. So long as it depends upon special instructors it will not be a real success.

Miss Sibyl Howe Avery, Teacher Physical Training, High School, Providence, R. I.:

In the English High School (600 girls, one teacher) there are two twenty-minutes periods per week; girls wear street dresses and basement playroom is used as a gymnasium. There are voluntary after-school classes where gymnasium suits are required. In addition to regular gymnasium work (Sargent system), there are many games; basket ball is a favorite and the number of players is growing. The boys have very little gymnastics. There are two high school football teams. Three of the four high schools have some physical training. The subject, however, is treated inadequately from lack of time and scant money appropriations.

STATE OF CONNECTICUT.*

Hon. C. D. Hine, State Secretary of Education:

Most city schools have simple gymnastics but few undertake systematic physical culture. The only way of

* Publishes a little state manual on physiology, hygiene etc., with some suggestions on exercise.

securing good physical training in all schools would be to have supervision. We cannot secure experts in all the schools. We, therefore, need supervisors to direct the work. It is not a subject required by law.

C. N. Kendall, Superintendent of Schools, New Haven, Conn.:

I send you a copy of a pamphlet, a manual of exercises, prepared by Dr. E. A. Arnold of the Anderson School of Gymnastics. It was arranged for teachers in our schools. I do not think the public in New Haven is especially interested one way or the other in physical training.

E. H. Smiley, Principal of High School, Hartford, Conn.:

The city's interest is shown by the fact that an ample gymnasium and two instructors, a gentleman and lady, have been furnished in the high school. There will probably be three periods per week (forty-five minutes each) for each pupil under competent instructor. Physical examinations are given preparatory to physical training. To extend such training over the state, instructor and time must be arranged for.

Edward G. Coy, Principal of Hotchkiss School, Lakeville, Conn.:

Attitude most friendly to different branches of athletics, baseball, football, tennis and track athletics. We seek best results from them as sports and educational agencies. Gymnasium and playground are under charge of an expert; teams are always under supervision. Violent exercise and undue competition are guarded against; games away from school grounds allowed only once a year. We believe athletic play valuable also in an intellectual and moral way. Boys would degenerate with no outlet for surplus energy and school life grow tame. Can hardly say how physical training may be extended in all public schools, because for its successful development it requires school spirit, which it is difficult to arouse in a public school.

Dr. Jay W. Seaver, Yale University Gymnasium:

In Yale academic department every member of freshman class is required to take gymnasium exercises from November 1 to April 1, unless connected with an athletic team in regular training. A physical examination precedes this gymnasium work. After examination a little book of prescribed exercises to meet individual needs is given to each student to guide him in exercise aside from class work. An instructor is on floor of gymnasium at all times to give any necessary suggestions, and a physician is present for free consultation on health five hours each day. A room is devoted to medical gymnastics for men needing special treatment for deformity, etc. The university assumes no responsibility for training of athletes. The gymnasium is equipped with all forms of baths and apparatus of German and American type.

Physical training can be introduced into public schools by interesting. teachers in the work in the normal schools and giving special inducements to teachers to study and apply gymnastics in their schools. The inducement may be by higher salary, for such a teacher is more valuable than otherwise. All cities should have a physical training director to organize the work. Where school boards will not hire such director, let individual teachers be encouraged to undertake the work and meantime school boards should be brought up to date.

NEW YORK CITY.

W. H. Maxwell, Superintendent of Schools:

My advice, based on experience, to any board of education or to any superintendent about to introduce physical culture, is to obtain a first-class supervisor or director of the subject, and to require him or her to train the class teachers to do the work.

PHILADELPHIA, PA.

Edward Brooks, Superintendent of Schools:

We have gymnastics in our schools. Many of our principals and teachers have made special preparation for physical exercises. We have a very superior course of physical training in our Girls' Normal School in which most of the teachers of the public schools are educated. It may be extended over the state by the thorough education of the teachers of the state.

United States Military Academy, West Point, N. Y.:

Colonel N. L. Mills, U. S. Army, Superintendent, forwards reply from Herman J. Koehler, Sword Master and Teacher of Gymnastics:

Methods of training are dependent upon existing conditions; what may be of value in one instance may be a failure in another. . . . All men are physically sound on entrance here. During the four years' course they are constantly under surveillance of surgeon; every minute of the day is marked out; hygienic conditions are as nearly perfect as science can make them. Food, water, bathing, clothing, ventilation, everything has been carefully considered and covered by regulations with penalty for disobedience. The individual has much to do with the above, but the amount of exercise is regulated entirely by the authorities.

Physical training begins instantly on arrival of cadet. Upper classmen teach military carriage and "setting up" exercises for months. These are not so much for physical development as for easy and graceful poise and carriage. Gymnasium work begins with the beginning of mental work. It aims at: 1. The promotion of bodily health; 2. To offset drain of severe application to mental studies; 3. Development of physical strength, endurance, alertness, agility and the mastery of the muscle system, which means gracefulness, ease of movement and precision.

The method is military in that it makes it possible to train many at one time, movements are only such as are beyond question beneficial and in which liability to injury or over-exertion is reduced to a minimum. The means employed are well equipped gymnasium, interest of student and rigid discipline. The work is systematic and progressive, embracing everything from setting up exercises to usual gymnastic appliances and including, besides, fencing and swimming. Forty-five minutes daily are given to this work in the first year. If measurements are below standard more time must be given. During the remaining three years riding and regular military drills take the place of gymnasium work and keep students in splendid physical condition. The cadet may be said to be constantly in training.

The time is fast approaching when those in charge of public education will find it absolutely impossible to longer disregard the bodies of the children intrusted to their care. The matter has been too long neglected as is apparent to all who take even a passive interest in our school children. We have been too much engrossed in other matters and have given the education of our children too little thought, permitting those who have made teaching a profession to do very much as they saw fit. It is to be regretted that educators have not felt the responsibility which has thus been placed upon their shoulders. That, however, is readily accounted for by the fact that teaching with some is, in by far too many cases, but a makeshift, to be gladly dropped when some other opportunities present themselves. Hearty coöperation of educators of the right stamp is needed. Men holding the purse strings of public education should accede to the demand of those in a position to judge in these matters.

In ordinary public schools it would be impossible to have anything but the simplest methods, usually that of exercising between desks. However, (I can say from experience) even here much good can be accomplished. In future every school erected should have a gymnasium of suitable size. This entails little expense and would be a blessing to the children. Where schools are already erected, special gymnasium buildings for the children of two or three adjacent districts are recommended. This is done in some German cities.

The work should be in charge of a superintendent of physical education, assisted by a competent corps of instructors. These should give all instruction, class teachers having nothing to do with this instruction. It is often the case (and I again speak from experience) that physical education has failed in our public schools because its success was dependent upon class teachers who were either neglectful or incompetent. It is a profession by itself and it is a mistake to think that any man who has not been properly trained for this special purpose can conduct it properly.

REMARKS ON LETTERS.

The correlation of physical training to public education is sought because essential to a wise system of public instruction. Such a system is created to advance the power and happiness of the individual and the race. An education which ignores or impairs the body is not properly education.

The inquiry, herewith presented, shows that profound interest in physical training exists in some parts of New England, in others it receives scant attention and in many places it is ignored. This form of training may be enriched by contributions from hand work, voice, training, music, right intellectual pursuits and good morals. In truth every part of knowledge is related to every other part. A larger number of male teachers will probably be required to effect needed changes. Boys, at least, should have more service from men in all stages

of training. The last word has not been said on school curricula. They are mostly new and comparatively experimental. The fact that physical training is recognized in but few, is absent from or simply squeezed into many schools, suggests needed revision at some points. Let leading schools and colleges invest the subject with proper dignity and value. If not of the first importance, as many think, for the physical life is the basis and instrument of the intellectual and moral life, it claims at least equal rank with any other school subject. Much may thus be accomplished. Legal recognition by state laws, believed by Secretary Hill to be involved in a proper interpretation of present statutes, will naturally follow in reasonable ways.

Questions of working plans may readily be adjusted, as with any school subject, by men competent to handle the teaching and economic sides of the subject. Present conditions lift to undue preëminence the military school which gives ceaseless care to physique as a requisite for successful war. The school of the people which is designed to conserve and develop society in a sane and rational way must not be thus left behind.

This inquiry reveals the need of conference among those directly concerned in the administration of education. Public education in New England is too vital a matter to be conducted in a divisive fashion or left to grope its way. Wise direction, concerted action and organized effort are necessary to advance this and other school and social interests.

Broadly trained teachers of physical culture may take the initiative in this work. They will be reinforced by the medical profession, parents, leaders in education and public opinion. Schools will not be slow to respond. Physical training needs to be better interpreted to the public mind. It has playground and gymnasium, but it is far more than these. It has been too much thought a matter of luxury and recreation merely, but it goes deeper into life. Man is a unity; there is a solidarity throughout his nature. There is an interplay and interpenetration of mind and body. A developed physique, hand-work, intellectual pursuits, trained will, moral purpose are inseparable. They are confederate in building a sane and symmetrical manhood. Let them keep step and time. Thus alone shall the school be true to life and fulfil its function in civilization. The right training of the youth is the renovation of the world and the resurrection of the race.

DISCUSSION.

Dr. D. A. Sargent of Harvard University said he agreed with the views of the paper as to the necessity of physical training in all New England schools. The facts presented show that the subject, while of vital importance, has generally inadequate treatment. It is evident that this interest needs to be considered in a wiser spirit and a more comprehensive way than it now receives. A generation or less ago, when the population was less urban, most youth, especially in the country, found much exercise in their necessary work, as in swinging the axe, riding the horse and varied forms of labor. But under the changed conditions of life new provisions are imperative if the physique of the people is preserved and improved. A duty evidently rests on teachers of physical training, educational leaders, parents and citizens generally to lift the whole subject to the high plane its importance commands. Examinations show that among students the physical development of males is superior to that of females, and that in many cases the sanitary state of school properties is defective. Numerous facts might be adduced to show how strong a claim the subject presented has on public attention.

Professor W. T. Sedgwick of the Massachusetts Institute of Technology said that the New England Education League was doing good service in calling attention to the fact that the people of New England are one population group, and that so fundamental a subject as education should have broader treatment than it has received. Speaking as a biologist, this population group is one organism with metropolis and cities as heart and nerve centres vitally joined to their outlying areas. It is not worthy of New England civilization to have the existing differences in educational privileges between country and city, town and town, state and state, continned where they can be remedied.

As to physical training, it is one of a number of things which should be introduced in all schools. In order to effect this result, a better public opinion must be formed, for the system of education rests on the intelligent support of the people. It is also necessary that greater harmony of view be secured as to the first principles in physical training, and the method of procedure in carrying forward such training. This will give a rational, scientific and effective kind of training. Some communities have done much for playgrounds, gymnasia and physical care of pupils, but a large number are grossly neglecting these important features of school life.

School hygiene is a subject which should have a large place in public thought, and in the estimation of teachers. It touches personal and social welfare and affects the vigor of the individual and the race.

PAPERS ON PHYSICAL TRAINING.

The following papers were submitted to the Boston Physical Education Society in connection with foregoing address:

To State Secretaries and State Boards of Education, Mayors and School Boards of Cities and Town School Committees of New England:

The undersigned, who are interested in the physical training of children and youth in our schools, both public and private, and in improved physical conditions of school buildings, out-buildings and grounds, respectfully recognize your leadership in promoting these important objects, and solicit, where possible, more vigorous effort in behalf of these interests.

We recognize with satisfaction that at some points in New England much effort has been made to secure good health and right physical development of pupils and proper sanitary conditions in school life. An investigation recently made into these matters and correspondence with leading superintendents, principals and others in New England show, however, that too often these interests receive very slight attention or are wholly neglected.

The relation of right physical training and surroundings during school life to the health, growth, intellectual and moral life and after-career of all pupils is generally conceded. Facilities for such training are not expensive, but the non-recognition of its importance has resulted in its entire or partial neglect in many schools. Other studies and subjects of value, but of less relative importance, have frequently crowded this fundamental interest into narrow limits in some places, or have prevented its entrance into school life in other communities.

School playrooms, playgrounds and athletic fields are too rarely given their due prominence in the arrangement of schools, to the detriment of children and youth who lose opportunities for physical exercise and the discipline and pleasure of innocent youthful sports. In no city has the system of parks and public playgrounds been brought into right relations to the school system.

Attention has frequently been called by school men, medical men and others to the need of better care in schools as to adjustment of school furniture to the pupil, the light, ventilation, mid-day lunch, pressure of studies, physical examinations, water or baths on school premises, out-buildings. In certain New England communities much progress has been made in all these matters, but, as has been said, an extensive investigation shows that much remains to be done to secure right conditions generally. It would be possible to name communities where these interests are receiving due attention from school management and the public, and, also, to specify communities where they are grossly neglected, but such specification is not our purpose. We aim rather to secure, so far as possible, better general school conditions throughout all New England. These results, it is thought, do not of necessity involve increased cost, but greater care.

The neglect of physique and proper sanitation in schools has a pernicious effect upon society at large. It leads to neglect in these matters on the part of adults and to lack of care of public health, sanitary conditions of homes and communities and retards social progress. It gives to the military school, which trains for war and which practises ceaseless care of the physique, a disproportionate place in public training. To the advancement of the individual, family and community physical vigor and education are essential. Both of these conditions may be promoted to a greater extent by right training in the schools of the people.

Your leadership in the lines indicated is gratefully acknowledged. It has been necessary to progress already made and will promote further improvement, both in progressive and backward communities. In all wise efforts to advance these interests it is our conviction that the public will give support and coöperation, to the end that in all New England conditions in and about the school may be favorable to the training of a strong, self-reliant and progressive people.

PAPER II.

To the President and Fellows of Harvard College:

We, the undersigned, respectfully submit to you the following petition:

That physical training be admitted to the same rank with other college subjects which require the same time in and out of class or lecture room, and allowed to count in like manner for college standing and degree.

We, also, beg leave to ask your favorable attention to the considerations herewith stated:

1. The value of physical training, rightly conducted, to the health, vigor, intellectual and moral life of the student and his after-career is generally conceded.

2. The facilities for such training at Harvard College in buildings, appliances, grounds and instruction are abundant and excellent.

3. These facilities, provided by persons interested in right education, will, it is believed, be more productive if the college raises this interest to the same plane and dignity with other college pursuits.

4. Physical training and related subjects, without such recognition, are regarded by students and the public as of lower rank, recreations or luxuries, to the detriment of the student and the cause of symmetrical education, and in numerous cases are crowded out of the courses of students by other studies and various other considerations, which would be removed if a higher estimate were put on this department in college administration.

5. The influence of college education on society is narrowed as compared with the military school, which gives ceaseless attention to physique, a defect in college training, in the opinion of many, to the disadvantage of the college man, college and society.

6. All lower schools, especially secondary schools, which are much affected by the example and opinion of the college, share in the detriment referred to, and those who have them in charge fail to find in the college the suggestion and reinforcement desirable for the best results in physical education, physical conditions and environment of schools.

7. The contribution of the college to the life of the people is less than would be forthcoming, if the college in its administration placed this subject in better relation to the general training of youth.

8. The action to which your petitioners solicit your favorable consideration would, in their opinion, be justified on educational grounds, would commend itself to parents and guardians of youth and to all interested in a well-balanced education.

CPSIA information can be obtained
at www.ICGtesting.com
Printed in the USA
BVHW041025210219
540828BV00009B/137/P